# HOW TO BE A $UCCESSFUL
# FAMILY LIFE EDUCATOR:

## Marketing Yourself and Your Programs

Linda Blend Petruolo, CFLE, CCFE

Library of Congress Control Number: 2001119218
ISBN 0-9714934-0-5

Cover, illustrations, layout designed by Susan Fecho.

# DEDICATION

This book is dedicated to all the
Family Life Educators,
who are committed to making a difference
in the lives
of individuals and families.

## To My Own Family

My husband and my friend,
Rocco Petruolo,
who not only believes in me, but
teaches me how to think
*out-of-the-box*.

My children,
Andrew and Samantha Rose,
my pride and joy.

# ACKNOWLEDGMENTS

A Heartfelt Thank You

**Pauline Gross, Ph.D.,**
former professor and role model,
who encouraged and inspired me
through her dedication
to her students and to the field of
Family Life Education.

**Dawn Cassidy, M.Ed., CFLE.,**
Certification Director for the
National Council on Family Relations,
who supported my projects from the beginning,
offering guidance and encouragement.

**Susan Fecho, M.F.A.**
"The Computer Angel" - You saw my vision and helped
make it come alive through support as artist
and graphic designer.

# Table of Contents

# WHERE THERE IS NO VISION,

# THE PEOPLE PERISH ...

*Proverbs 29:18*

# INTRODUCTION

In today's job market, Family Life Educators are in need of not only encouragement, but also concrete and practical skills to help create, carve and maintain their rightful place among other family-oriented professionals.

Specifically designed for Family Life Educators, this book provides the vital information you need to market your programs and the field of Family Life Education. Packed with real-life, entertaining stories, practical advice and tested marketing strategies, this book will help you break through the "invisibility barrier" and gain the professional recognition you rightfully deserve!

Part One

# FAMILY LIFE EDUCATION:
## A BUSINESS LIKE NO OTHER!

Frustrated? Discouraged? Is this how you feel when you try to explain Family Life Education to people? Do they look at you with a clueless expression when you say you are a Family Life Educator?

Let me share a recent experience with you. It was the day the proverbial straw broke the camel's back. I walked into the local coffee shop for my daily cappuccino, when the owner (a former Nurse, whom I had previously educated about the profession of Family Life Education) pointed to two women sitting at a nearby table.

I approached these two health professionals about possibly offering my programs at their organization. The conversation went something like this:

> Me: "Hello, ladies. My name is Linda Petruolo.
> I am a Certified Family Life Educator.
> I was told you work at ...."

**(Lesson: Network.)**

These friendly ladies nodded eagerly. They introduced themselves as Caroline and Pam. Both worked at a local mental health facility. Caroline was a Social Worker, and Pam worked in Human Resources.

> Me: "I haven't lived in this area very long.
> Could you tell more about your organization?

### (Lesson: Gather information.)

Caroline and Pam took turns describing the facility, the staff and the clientele.

The conversation continued, and I briefly described Family Life Education programs I had already designed and implemented.

Caroline and Pam still listened, smiled and nodded appropriately until asked if such programs were offered at their facility:

> Pam: "You're a what?... A...(pause)...family...(pause)...
>
> Me: "A Certified Family Life Educator," I repeated.

Surely they knew what I was talking about. I had just spent the last few minutes talking about programs. They even nodded and smiled! Something was wrong -- I felt it in my guts!

### (Lesson: Never underestimate your intuition.)

Pam still looked puzzled. Suddenly her friend piped up:

> Caroline: "Oh, I know what that is," she said with a knowing smile and looked directly at her friend.
>
> "They teach skills to the intellectually challenged ... (pause) ... you know ... like sorting laundry and buying groceries."

I felt like I was just punched in the stomach. Her answer literally knocked the wind out of me. This was definitely an example of "the blind leading the blind."

Recovering from this invisible blow, I explained the difference between the two professions. I then offered my business card and brochure, stating that I would be in touch with them later that week.

***(Lesson: Think on your feet.)***

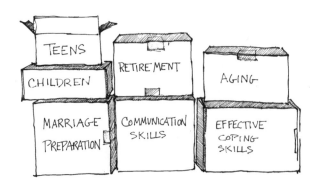

# FAMILY LIFE EDUCATION:
## THREE SIMPLE WORDS

### FAMILY

The family, in all its diversity, still plays a crucial and vital role in shaping lives. Most of us have had a mother, father, siblings, grandparents, aunts, cousins at some point along the way. In general, we aren't just hatched and left to fend for ourselves like turtles. To the best of my knowledge, the family is still recognized as a major agent of socialization.

### LIFE

Although the mystery and purpose of it has led to many a scientific, philosophical and religious debate, we would, however, like to believe that most professionals have all experienced several stages of the life cycle by now. For some individuals, it is a journey filled with constant obstacles and challenges; others appear to sail through it without a hitch; some claim not to even have one; and while others seem to re-visit adolescence once a mid-life crisis occurs. Nonetheless, we all still go down this path at least once.

### EDUCATION

Street-smart, book-smart, home-schooled or sandbox-smart, have we not all been exposed to the concept of education at some point? Our *family* educates us. *Life* educates us. Every single choice we make may be interpreted as a learning experience, complete with its own unique set of consequences that we can either learn from or ignore. In effect, the choices we make dictate the lives we lead.

Three ordinary, household words strung together -- simple enough? Apparently not. I'll dare ask you again: Why don't people know what Family Life Education is?

***(Lesson:  Never assume.)***

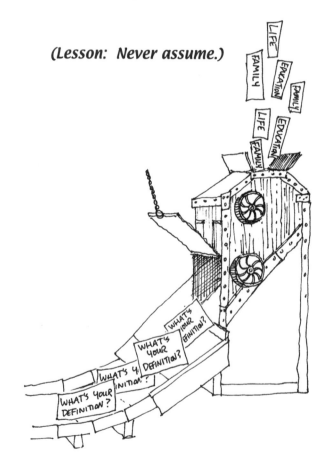

How to be a Successful Family Life Educator

# FAMILY LIFE EDUCATION:
## WHAT'S YOUR DEFINITION?

If you pause, sigh, and roll your eyes skyward when someone asks you what Family Life Education is, you might suspect there is a problem.  But, when you start by answering, "Uh, well ... it's kinda-sorta-like..,"  then you *really know* there is a problem!

As a Family Life Educator, you may agree that defining our profession may be one of the most difficult tasks we have. Leaders in the field of Family Life Education have spent the past forty years working on a definition. Arcus et al. (1993) provide, in chronological order, the various definitions of Family Life Education.

Considering the very essence of Family Life Education, it is far from easy to capture one perfect "catch-all" definition. Both Arcus et. al. (1993) and Powell and Cassidy (2000) enlighten us to the fact that many of the field's leading specialists agreed that the great debate over a definition, may not only have led to confusion, but also wasted time vis-à-vis progression of the field.

Although the one "final and definite definition" is not quite in yet, the National Council on Family Relations offers the following definition for certification:

> Family life education provides skills for individuals and families to lead productive and satisfying lives.
>
> It includes knowledge about how families work; the interelationship of families and society; human growth and development throughout the life span; the physiological and psychological aspects of human sexuality; the impact of money and time management on daily family life; the importance and value of parent education; the effects of policy and legislation on families; ethical considerations in professional conduct; and a solid understanding and knowledge of how to teach and/or develop curriculum for what are often sensitive and personal issues.

This definition seems to be thorough and all encompassing, yet, why does the first paragraph make me think of the coffeeshop incident I mentioned earlier?

What definition do you offer? Here is a list of keywords that may prove helpful in establishing your own comfortable, working definition:

- empower
- individuals
- families
- group discussions

- enrich
- lifespan
- education
- skills
- focus
- prevention
- well-being

*(Lesson: Don't risk being caught off-guard.*
*Prepare a short, working definition.)*

# FAMILY LIFE EDUCATION:
## THE KEY FEATURES

Even though the dust has not yet settled around the definition issue, the good news is that there is consensus about "key features" specific to Family Life Education.

To summarize Arcus (1993) and Powell and Cassidy (2000), as Family Life Educators, our work is relevant to, and should focus on, the various needs of individuals and families across the lifespan; in our various settings, we should offer an educational rather than therapeutic approach, being mindful of differing family values; and we are to be qualified and knowledgeable of the multidisciplinary areas of Family Life Education, and cognizant of its goals.

Although this summary may read like a "Family Life Educator's Pledge of Allegiance," the major points have been clearly outlined.

*(Lesson: Understand the ground rules.)*

# FAMILY LIFE EDUCATION:
## LIMITS AND BOUNDARIES

From a Family Life Education perspective, we are to keep the "different dimensions of learning" (Arcus, 1993), at the forefront. Assisting individuals and families to:

- gain knowledge
- explore attitudes and values
- develop interpersonal skills

are the major components we should focus upon.

Always keep in mind that we are Family Life Educators, not Therapists. It is imperative for us to practice within ethical and professional parameters, taking heed not to overstep these boundaries. For the most part, our orientation deals with the "here and now" behavior (Gross, 1985) and "it is important for the educator to make the distinction. Education is oriented toward the healthy factors of the personality ..." As Family Life Educators, our aim is not curative (reducing social or psychological dysfunctions), but rather, preventive and growth-oriented.

Doherty (1995) provides a structured and well-defined, 5-tiered model on levels of family involvement. Family Life

Education should be restricted to the lower three levels of involvement, whereas, the higher levels are to be reserved for the trained and skilled Family Therapists, who are better qualified to deal with more complex issues.

Level 1: Minimal Emphasis on Family
Level 2: Information and Advice
Level 3: Feelings and Support
Level 4: Brief Focused Intervention
Level 5: Family Therapy

Doherty's framework on competency levels of family involvement serves as a useful tool in assisting us to make that distinction, especially when fine-lines get blurred, and issues are to be addressed.

> An effective family life educator will recognize issues that go beyond the scope of family life education, and be prepared to provide referrals to more appropriate professionals and resources.
>
> Powell and Cassidy (2000)

Attempting to practice beyond your level of competence is treading on dangerous ground, risking the possibility of doing more harm than good.

*(Lesson: Know and accept your level of competency.)*

How to be a Successful Family Life Educator

# PREVENTION

*Can Family Life Education make a difference in people's lives?*

I would say a definite **YES** to that! The world is changing, and will continue to do so. Every generation has its own set of social changes. Each change brings with it a myriad of social problems for individuals and families to deal with.

As Family Life Educators, we can not do anything about the social changes per se -- however, through education, we can, and do assist these very individuals and families (yes, while they are still reasonably "healthy", and still reasonably "well-functioning") -- to better cope with the resulting problems that they encounter.

Agreed, that means **before they are in crisis**. Therefore, it is safe to say that preventive mental health is the very essence of Family Life Education.

According to Darling (1987), "family life education is perceived ... as the foremost preventive measure for the avoidance of family problems." As well, the experts seemed to agree that the raison d'être, focus and goal of family life education was "to strengthen and enrich individual and family well-being" (Arcus et al., 1993, p. 12).

> **Family Life Education promotes preventive mental health and well-being.**

## THE IMPORTANT ROLE OF PREVENTION

Without a doubt, over time, life's stressors can take their toll on individuals and families. Keep in mind that we all have our own personal tolerance level for stress. When pressing issues are addressed and dealt with in a timely and effective manner, everyone benefits.

But, too many out there suffer from *M.M.M.S.*, a sad, unnecessary and unfortunate disease that debilitates - and the long-term effects can prove to be devastating!

*M.M.M.S* = *M*edical *M*odel *M*indset *S*yndrome. (Remember that you heard it here first, I coined the phrase!) Our society has been programmed to believe in the 'medical model' with its believed premise of "if it ain't broke, don't fix it!" Fortunately, there is a cure, but like everything else, people have to "buy into it".

-Do individuals and families really have to wait until they "break down"?

-Must they wait to be in a crisis situation?

*I don't think so!* This is no longer necessary.

As Family Life Educators, we are available to help. How do we help? Through educational methodologies such as "group discussion, lecturette, role play, and film ..." (Gross, 1985).

When skills are mastered and competency grows, self-esteem increases -- and this has a positive effect on the continued healthy functioning of the individual. Since the family works as a unit -- you may infer that healthy self-esteem reflects onto the family, and in turn promotes its level of functioning.

It is best summed up in an interview I did a few years ago:

> "Information is knowledge and knowledge is power ... Power is the ability to respond effectively and appropriately. Once you understand that equation, it's limitless... We can assist people learn to deal with situations before they become unmanageable ... There is a light at the end of the tunnel; we help people learn that they have the power within themselves." *The Review*, March 6, 1996

## WHEN A PREVENTIVE APPROACH IS RESISTED

When individuals *resist* a preventive approach, they can sometimes find themselves falling deeper and deeper into an abyss. At this stage, recovery may indeed be slow, lengthy, and costly.

It would appear that when the individual can no longer cope, and in fact is recognized as "broken," that there is a frenzy to seek help. Visits to Doctors' offices and Emergency Rooms soon become the norm. Waiting rooms get crowded with non-urgent, non-medical cases. The waiting time is increased. Other patients' time is wasted. All this may have been avoided if the person had a **preventive-oriented mindset.**

Now, "the heavies" are sometimes obliged to get involved: the psychologists, the psychiatrists, the psychiatric social workers, youth protection officials, domestic violence workers, substance abuse counselors, juvenile courts, lawyers, public defenders, district attorneys, probation officers, and judges. As yet, I still haven't mentioned the traumatizing effects on immediate family members. Friends, neighbors, extended families, and employers are also affected, each in their own manner.

One would assume that it may, in fact, not only prove to be more cost-effective, but, moreover, more cost-efficient for government and businesses to hire Family Life Educators to assist individuals with basic interpersonal, communication and coping skills.

## PREVENTION: THE BOTTOM LINE

-Could individuals and families benefit from a
preventive health and mental health mindset? **Yes.**

-Should our youth be educated as to preventive vs.
non-preventive mindsets? **Yes.**

-Could millions of healthcare tax dollars be saved
when both Americans and Canadians change to a
healthier, preventive-oriented lifestyle? **Yes.**

# THE IMPORTANCE OF CERTIFICATION:
## MAY I SEE YOUR CREDENTIALS, MA'AM?

Many Family Life Educators pursue Certification from either the National Council on Family Relations (NCFR) or Family Service Canada (FSC). Both of these organizations have specific standards and criteria for their Certification Program.

Family Life Educators applying to either program are **choosing** to be put under the microscope before the respective Certification Committee's watchful eye. Applicants undergo a thorough and rigorous screening process.

### THE NATIONAL COUNCIL OF FAMILY RELATIONS

According to the NCFR's *Standards and Criteria for the Certified Family Life Educator Program (CFLE)*, evidence of a minimum of 2 years of experience must be provided by those with a family-related degree. Five years of experience is required of those with a non-family degree. All applicants must have at least a bachelor's degree. Supporting documentation of appropriate academic preparation, professional development and work experience in each of these ten family life substance areas is required:

1. Families in Society
2. Internal Dynamics of Families
3. Human Growth and Development over the Life Span
4. Human Sexuality
5. Interpersonal Relationships
6. Family Resource Management
7. Parent Eduction and Guidance
8. Family Law and Public Policy
9. Ethics
10. Family Life Education Methodology

Letters of recommendation attesting to essential basic personal characteristics, (such as ethical behavior and respect for others), as well as personal qualities (such as flexibility, maturity, awareness of personal cultural attitudes and values, self-confidence, and emotional stability, etc.) are also sought. Intellectual, social, verbal and written skills are also reviewed. Certification is valid for a period of five years, after which you may apply for Re-Certification.

Re-Certification is an entirely different process requiring different application forms. This time, supporting evidence of continuing educational activity is required, in at least 2 of the ten family life substance areas. To qualify, you must accumulate proof of 100 contact hours.

## FAMILY SERVICE CANADA

Family Service Canada offers a Certification program that is similar to the NCFR. The legal designation of Certified Canadian Family Educator (CCFE) is granted to those who submit proof of at least one year of training and experience and show evidence of education, professional development, training and work experience in nine family life substance areas. These categories include:

1. Orientation to Family Education
2. Individual, life stage and family development
3. Families
4. Human Sexuality
5. Interpersonal Relationships
6. Social Attitude
7. Values Education
8. Group Process
9. Program Planning

As with the NCFR, letters of recommendation are also sought. Details of essential personal characteristics and qualities, intellectual, social, verbal and written skills are to be provided, and are reviewed by the Certification Committee. Certification is valid for a period of five years. Re-Certification is yet another process which may be applied for. Candidates are then reviewed by the Re-Certification Committee and are approved if they meet the criteria.

Both the NCFR and FSC are organizations that promote, encourage and support continuing education and professional development.

## WHY BE CERTIFIED?

Certification is not mandatory - we volunteer - no one twists our arms. In business terminology, it would be considered quality assurance, a controlled process aimed at protecting the consumer by assuring quality. We are inspected for quality and given the seal of approval.

> Certification grants recognition to individuals who have met defined qualifications," and "... it is a credential indicating expertise in the field of family life education. (NCFR, 2000)

As Certified Family Life Educators, certification is something we value. It is something we strive for. It is highly-regarded within our profession. It is something to take pride in! Because of stringent criteria from organizations like the NCFR and FSC, Certification is slowly being recognized and accepted outside the field of Family Life Education. I would venture to say that it would most probably be one of the requirements for licensure in the future.

As Certified Family Life Educators, we remain determined and dedicated to making a difference in the lives of individuals and families. We *choose* to continuously challenge and upgrade our knowledge, rather than stagnate in our mire!

Certification packages may be obtained from:

National Council on Family Relations
Tel: 1-888-781-9331
E-Mail: ncfr3989@ncfr.org

Family Service Canada
Sylvie M. Charron, Executive Assistant
Tel: 1-613-722-9006
E-Mail: sm.charron@familyservicecanada.org

*(Lesson: Certification - GO FOR IT!)*

# SUCH IS LIFE -- FOR NOW, ANYWAY

Although Family Life Education has come a long way, it still has a way to go. For the time being, the unfortunate reality we all face is that we are not yet licensed -- which sadly translates into not being widely recognized. Licensure is a future possibility, but that is a state-by-state decision and process, complete with its own set of qualifications and criteria.

As Family Life Educators, even Certified ones, we soon find ourselves obliged to be "our own advocates," states NCFR Certification Director, Dawn Cassidy, and we quickly realize that we must not only "sell the concept of family life education," but also "our qualifications to potential employers" (NCFR NETWORK, Summer 1999). As many of you might agree, there certainly are not many jobs for Family Life Educators listed in the classifieds.

If no one knows who we are, or what our skills are, then how can we even expect to be acknowledged, respected or recognized as professionals!

Both L'Abate (1990) and Doherty (1995) suggest that Family Life Educators work hand-in-hand with other professionals, such as Family Therapists. L'Abate suggests that clients,

How to be a Successful Family Life Educator

once triaged as to a functionality-to-dysfunctionality continuum, be directed to the appropriate professional. Doherty mentions common issues that unavoidably overlap, and the need to work collaboratively -- pulling it all together -- for the client's sake. I could not agree more!

These specialists espouse truly superb and altruistic ideologies; however, with all due respect, I ask:

- Do the various other mental health professionals, such as social workers, family therapists or counselors, **really** work collaboratively with Family Life Educators?

- Do these same professionals reciprocate vis-à -vis clientele?

- Do these same professionals make referrals to Family Life Educators? And if so, how many referrals have **YOU** received lately?

- Do these same professionals believe that we are not qualified? (perhaps because we are not yet licensed?)

Or, on the other hand,

- Do these same professionals feel threatened by Family Life Educators? Do they perhaps feel that we are moving in on their territory?

As Family Life Educators, we focus on the "at-risk" rather than the "in-crisis" population. And, although we are really not considered behavioral health providers, the reality is that we are, in fact, qualified to provide education in building strengths - whether communication skills, interpersonal skills or effective coping strategies.

Unfortunately, even though we work within these clear-cut parameters, we do live in the real world, where egos, personalities, competition and money are all real issues. **Think about it.**

# OH, THE TOPICS THEY'LL HAVE
# AND THE PEOPLE YOU'LL SEE!

We are truly blessed! The NCFR's *Framework for Life-Span Family Life Education* (1997a), is an invaluable resource tool. At a glance, the major dimensions of Family Life Education content are categorized and detailed.

I have heard colleagues complain that they are bored with the "same old programs". In all honesty, taking into consideration the ages of the lifespan, topic areas and content that we have to work with, can we really be at a loss of material for designing programs? *I think not.* I offer suggestions for them to perhaps get more creative and diverse in regards to both the content and in teaching methodologies.

From babies to *bubbies*, and everyone in between, Family Life Education allows us the freedom to explore and expand our own horizons. Enjoy and appreciate your clients -- each group creates its own energy -- no two groups are exactly alike. Let's not forget that learning is a life long process. Just because we are the Educators doesn't mean we can't learn. To the contrary. Learning is two-way, advocates Gross (1985): "... both the educator and participants have something to contribute to the group, and that each can learn from the other."

### *(Lesson: Expand your horizons.)*

# YOU DON'T KNOW WHAT YOU'VE GOT
## ... TILL IT'S GONE

Louise, a fellow Family Life Educator, frustrated with the struggle of constantly having to be her own advocate, decided to change career paths. She signed up for the Social Work program at a prestigious university. The program was demanding, but "do-able" since about 80% of the course content overlapped with the Family Life Education program we had taken together. She did the work and the field placements and the transition into Social Work went smoothly.

Finding a job was the easy part all she had to do was look in the classified ads. She quickly found a job at a nearby hospital. She never had to explain her new career to family and friends, because everybody knew what a Social Worker was. Louise was happy.

Well, the days and the weeks and the months went by, and Louise started complaining that she felt stuck in a rut. Her days were filled with repetitive paperwork - completing forms for chronic patients, who were awaiting placement. Although she liked working with the families, her work did not allow for creativity, nor independence, nor imagination, nor freedom to re-design her work, nor the opportunity for learning from others during open forum group discussions.

How to be a Successful Family Life Educator

Louise soon became restless. She claimed that she felt stifled. Her work no longer provided that medium where she could be creative, imaginative, and independent. Her environment was stifling, and she soon found it to be psychologically debilitating. Louise was not as happy as she thought she would be in her new career.

Louise's hospital contract was soon up for renewal. After seriously reviewing the pros and the cons, Louise decided not to return to the hospital. She finally admitted that she missed being a Family Life Educator. She missed the small group interaction; she missed the creative juices flowing. But most of all, she missed the freedom of designing and implementing her own workshops in the community - even if it meant being her own advocate once again.

Part Two

# PROVIDING THE "MISSING LINK"
## IN THE FAMILY LIFE EDUCATION
## CURRICULUM

Basically, we all received the same formal education and training in Family Life Education. However, there were no courses offered in promoting the field of Family Life Education. Nor were there any courses in marketing yourself and your programs. **Hence**, this book on these very subjects.

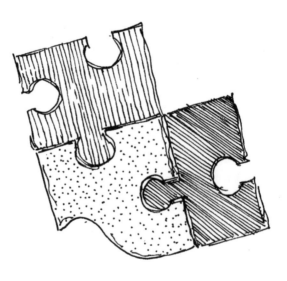

# ..THE STUFF THEY NEVER
# TAUGHT IN CLASS

In retrospect, it all began when friends started asking me:

> How come I was getting offers to do workshops -
> **when they couldn't even give theirs away for free?**

> Why was I limiting seating to workshops -
> **when they had trouble filling the first row of seats?**

> Why was I getting media attention from local
> newspaper editors and local television stations -
> **when they were paying big bucks for advertising?**

They just wanted to know why.

- Did I have a higher I.Q. than my peers?
  *I don't think so.*

- Was I a beauty queen with flowing hair and
  legs up to there.
  *No, not me!*

- Did I possess super-human powers?
  *Heck no!*

I was just your average, forty-something, married, neurotic, overweight, stressed, mother of two teens kind-of-person, who, sorry to say, possessed no secret or magical powers. But, I was a woman with a mission -- one that proved not to be impossible.

What did I know about marketing Family Life Education? Not much! I knew about families, interpersonal and group dynamics, leadership skills, but definitely **not** marketing. This topic was never covered in class. I learned the hard way - through trial and error.

Initially, the cost in terms of time, energy and money was substantial. I was investing a lot, but getting **bubkes** in return. Finally, a little research and development paid off. I developed a marketing plan that started getting the results I wanted. Before long, colleagues were asking me for tips on marketing strategies.

*(Lesson: Determination and perseverance are key qualities. )*

# DEVELOPING A MARKETING PLAN

**STOP THE PRESSES!** Before you start printing up those fliers and brochures, you first have to develop a marketing plan. This starts with *identifying* your target audience. Major companies hire focus groups, marketing experts and spent B-I-G bucks to do this work. The good news is that YOU can manage to accomplish this on your own. Remember, everything is relative - you are not Proctor and Gamble targeting all housewives across America! As a Family Life Educator, you are targeting *specific* members of your community.

# YOUR TARGET AUDIENCE:
## WHO ARE THEY?

Start by asking yourself the following three very important questions. Your answers will give you a clue as to who to target:

1. What type of Family Life Education workshop are you offering?
2. Have you defined the workshop participants you are targeting?
3. Who is most likely to use and benefit from your program?

## MATCHMAKER ... MATCHMAKER

Defining a target audience is hard work, and has to be well-thought out in advance. If not, you will be wasting time, energy and a lot of advertising money on attracting either the wrong group for your workshop, or no group at all. In effect, you are playing matchmaker, attempting to hook up your Family Life Education program with the appropriate individuals who need it.

For instance, let's say you have a wonderful parenting program. One of the workshops is entitled: "Engaging Cooperation In Children." What target audience are you aiming for? Who would benefit the most from your program? Who would be most likely to attend?

- Daycare Workers?
- Parents? (single? low-income? married? double-income?)
- Teachers (pre-school? kindergarten? elementary? middle school?)

## YA GOTTA HAVE A PLAN

This is the first and most important step in developing a marketing plan. Regardless of who your target audience is, the same basic rules apply. A study in demographics is required. It involves effort and a little leg-work, such as researching pertinent data, then following up with some market testing. It will, however, prove to be well worth it in the long run (take my word on this one!).

Keep in mind that you want your groups to be homogeneous, which may not only mean in terms of topic area and content, but also in regard to social and economic factors. It is important for group members to be able to relate to each other.

The first step is defining who your audience is. Now we want to find out where they are.

# WHERE ARE THEY?

## MARKETING RESEARCH

The next part of your marketing plan involves conducting marketing research. Not only does it provide a wealth of information that you must narrow down, but it also proves to be an investment in yourself and your future as a successful Family Life Educator!

## CREATING A TARGET GROUP

First, let me assure you that this research can be done without an MBA. Now that you've figured out who your target audience is, you have to proceed to the next step.

It is a very important area that should neither be neglected, nor overlooked. This research provides direction that is measurable, and eliminates the guesswork as to who your clients are, as well as what **they** want from your program (not what you think they want).

## PRIMARY RESEARCH

Roll up your sleeves - you've got some work to do. Primary research is information that you gather from **direct sources** from potential workshop participants. Start by designing a one-page questionnaire or survey. Don't overload the page; if your questionnaire/survey is well-thought out, 12-15 questions should be enough. Also, make responding quick and easy, i.e. boxes that can be checkmarked. You might want to find out about things like sex, age, marital status, level of education; number of children, occupation, address or zip code, and interests.

Let's say you offer Parenting workshops - include questions geared towards that. For example, ask if they have a need for parenting workshops; the age groups of children they are having difficulty with; the distance from your workshop to where they live; whether daycare facilities are needed in order for them to attend, etc. You can mail out your surveys or do telephone surveys. If you don't have time to call yourself, you may consider hiring a student.

To clarify, let's use the "Engaging Cooperation in Children" workshop as an example.

Let's say that you chose Daycare Workers as the audience you want to target. The size of your sample group can be as small or as large as you want to make it. Design a questionnaire that is very well thought out! Do a telephone survey, or better still, bring in your questionnaires to several targeted Daycare Centers. You want to be able to do a comparative study.

## ENGAGING COOPERATION
From personal experience, I know that it is best to contact the Daycare Directors in advance. Ask if you can take just fifteen minutes of their staff's time. Schedule a specific date and time to visit. By doing this, you will not only save your-

self time and be in a better position to engage their cooperation, but you will also...

    1) Spark their interest in an upcoming program

    2) Introduce **YOURSELF**

    3) Get your questionnaires back right away

    4) Start analyzing the results right away

    5) Get going on the advertising!

## ANALYZING THE RESULTS

These representative samplings will enable you to determine what features and benefits appeal to your audience. Is it the topic area and content? The desire to improve skills and strategies? The small group interaction? The cost? The day and time your workshop takes place? The workshop location? The easy parking? The free refreshments?

Once the results are analyzed, you will have a clear-cut, visible roadmap indicating what works, what doesn't, and why. You will be aware of their specific needs and how to best incorporate them. By collecting such valuable information (beforehand), you will now be in a better position to:

- comprehend where your business comes from
- avoid marketing problems
- develop an effective advertising plan

Without going into details of the psychology of advertising (a 6-credit course in itself!), let me say that in order for your targeted individuals to sign up for your Family Life Education workshops, it is imperative that you fulfill their needs. So, find out what they want.

## SECONDARY RESEARCH

Secondary research is information that you gather from *indirect sources*. Since demographics hold the key to identifying specifics on your client base, the more pertinent information at your fingertips, the better your chances are of targeting the appropriate individuals. You may be offering more than one program, so think carefully about what information you want to obtain.

If you are planning a parenting workshop, you will need to collect statistics, reports, scientific studies, as well as media or public polls relating to children. There are many ways and means of collecting the information you need. Both government and non-government agencies are available to assist you with your statistics. Your local City Hall or Chamber of Commerce are also excellent resources. There is nothing wrong with doing some research on your own - try going on-line, or going to the local or university library.

*(Lesson: Marketing is easier when you get to know the rules.)*

# DESIRE
## IS THE FIRST STEP
## TOWARDS SUCCESS.

# PROMOTING FAMILY LIFE EDUCATION

How do you promote this profession?
How do you get people to attend your workshops?
What do you do that is different from what others do?

Now that you have a better understanding of the **who, where, what** and **why** of your target audience, it is time to start exploring the **how**.

Does your organization or agency have the necessary personnel to take care of such things? Or, are you, like many other Family Life Educators, required to promote your own programs? If so, don't panic. I'll help you through it.

First of all, you have to start taking aim. Serious aim. Measurable aim. Your marketing efforts may not hit the bull's eye on the first try, but this is normal and expected - so take it in stride. Practice, patience, perseverance and flexibility are some of the important assets when promoting Family Life Education.

Imagination and creativity are also essential elements, and play vital roles in terms of a successful Family Life Education marketing plan. Never in my life did I ever think I was creative! Once you adopt a creative mindset, you will absolutely surprise and amaze yourself with what you can come up with!

First of all, whether you choose to work for an agency, or work independently, as a family life educator entrepreneur, you must start thinking **out-of-the-box**.

How? By looking **BEYOND**. By seeing the invisible. By envisioning a goal and making it happen!  But first of all, you have to believe you can.

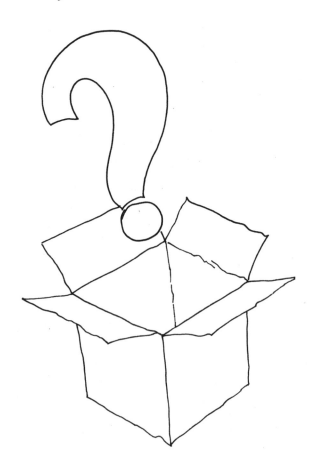

## Our Visions
### +
## Our Realities
### =
## The Dance Between the Two.

# ADVERTISING AND PACKAGING

For Family Life Educators, advertising is just one more task that they must become knowledgeable about, and learn to do themselves. If you work for an agency, you may be relieved of this chore (lucky you!)

Whether you know it or not, everything you wear, say and do may be interpreted as a form of advertising. How you dress in a meeting or when speaking publicly definitely says something about you. When it comes to Family Life Education, you and your program, are joined at the hip.

In our society, you are judged by how you look and how you act. You cannot make a first impression twice. Professionalism in dress and manner is imperative. What you show the public is of great importance. What do your wardrobe and grooming habits say about you? Sloppy or Professional? Wouldn't it be just wonderful to hire advertising and image-making people?

Even the place where you do business reflects on you. Take a good look around, and try to see things from a client's perspective.

- Is your office disorganized and messy?
  - What does this say about you?

- What about the room where you conduct your workshops?
  - Is the atmosphere conducive to learning?
  - Is it inviting?

Now, take a look at your letterhead, envelopes, and brochures. If you could describe them using just one word, what would that word be? Dull? Boring? Creative? Imaginative?

Once you know what your target audience wants, it is easier to design your advertising campaign around them. It's up to you to decide the what, where, how, and how much of it all -- and it's also up to you to keep on your toes. Whether you choose to advertise by direct mail, media kits, newspaper ads, hot-air balloons, or sky-writing, you are aiming for not only increased visibility, but also a **positive response** from the audience you are targeting.

Think about the importance of "**your total package**" and its effect on individuals. Can you think of anything that needs improving?

# MARKETING TOOLS AND STRATEGIES
## ... How Do You Get Them To Attend Your Workshops?

Marketing is about name recognition. There are numerous marketing tools at your disposal to let people know about you and your Family Life Education programs.

- What marketing tools are you presently using?
- How effective are they?
- Are you getting the results you anticipated?
- Are you keeping tabs of what works and what doesn't?

Whenever you decide to try something **new** or **different**, you also have to remember to track your results.

For the Family Life Education programs I have conducted over the years, I've experimented with a wide variety of marketing tools and strategies. You will soon notice that different ones appeal to different people. Therefore, it is wise to be knowledgeable about the many tools available to you. Always have at least one or two back-up plans -- so expand your marketing tool repertoire! Never limit yourself.

What works with one targeted group may, in fact, not be effective with another group. There are many factors involved in this, and I will not bore you with the psychology of it all, when it can be simplified by saying: different strokes for different folks. Take some time to find out what works with **your** targeted audience; then continue to use that winning formula.

*Let's check out some effective marketing tools and strategies right now!*

# DIRECT MAIL

*You guessed it!* As the name implies, direct mail involves mailing out *directly* to your targeted audience. Depending on your program, direct mail may prove to be an excellent advertising and marketing strategy for Family Life Educators.

## Your Direct Mail Package

To continue with a previous example, I will use the workshop on Engaging Cooperation in Children. You already decided that your target audience was Daycare Workers. Now, decide what marketing tools you want to use as part of your direct mailing.

- A brochure?
- A business card?
- A introductory type letter?
- A flier?

For your *first* mailing to the Daycare Workers, you may want to consider going all out and combine an introductory letter and a brochure. You may even clip it together with your business card on top. This plan may require more time and cost, but is a wonderful opportunity to introduce yourself. If you target the *same* Daycare Workers again, sending a brochure or flier is just fine - it can be sent in a matching envelope or just by itself, sealed with a small, transparent seal - the choice is yours!

Over the years, I have worked with the friendly and helpful staff at PaperDirect. They offer a great selection of quality, color-coordinated, theme-related speciality papers that can be purchased in small quantities. Their business cards, brochures, letterheads, envelopes and folders are great for direct mailings and media kits, so you may want to give them a call at 1-800-272-7377.

## Creating a Database

Are you equipped with a database of specific Daycare Workers that you want to send your direct mail package to? You may have already started creating your own database, using inexpensive tools such as the telephone book, Yellow Pages (never underestimate its potential!), Chamber of Commerce list, or even going on-line.

## House List

The list which **you** create is referred to as a House List, or In-House List. You are free to use your own lists over again for other direct market pieces you may want to distribute. Each Family Life Education program that you offer may be targeted to a different group of people. So, in effect, you may end up with several lists (which is very good!). It's best to keep your database as accurate as possible, which again, involves some effort. The work you put in now will most likely prove to be a very good investment later.

## List Brokers

On the other hand, if you do not have the time, nor the inclination to gather names and addresses, there are companies out there that offer such services (at a cost of course!). These companies can pretty well accommodate a request, no matter how large or small (although some companies have order minimums) and their staff can continually compile and update databases. If you wanted a list of all the Daycare Workers from coast to coast - they could oblige you. On the other hand, if you want to concentrate your efforts on locating Daycare Centers in your county, city or specific zip code, they can probably help you with that too.

## Mailing Houses

Many of these popular companies are now all encompassing and can assist you with every aspect of your direct-mail campaign. Not only can they obtain comprehensive lists, but also take care of the actual creating and mailing; everything from creating a brochure (with the help of their in-house graphic designer) to sealing envelopes, to applying appropriate postage, to even dropping your direct-mail package in their own mail boxes. Be forewarned, the more that is done for you, the more it will cost!

## Working Budget

Speaking of **costs**, how much budget do you have to spend on marketing and advertising? It is best to work out a realistic plan. Take the time to get a few price quotes for the same type of work. The more you do yourself, the better, **however**, if it is more cost-efficient to let the pros do the work, you may in fact, end up saving yourself some money in the long run. I know I did! (That subject is a book in itself!)

## Bulk Mail Rate

If direct-mailings are going to become a major part of your advertising strategy, go to your local post office and inquire if you qualify for a bulk rate permit. There is a yearly cost of about $70; however, if you plan on sending out about a thousand brochures, it will pay for itself in your first mailing alone! Be sure that the permit number is visible on each piece going out, otherwise it runs the risk of being rejected and re-routed back to you.

# BUSINESS CARDS

There once was a time when life was much simpler. A business card usually meant a small, rectangular, 3-1/2" x 2" usually white, quality stock, paper card that had information like your name, your title, your phone and fax number.

Nowadays, there exists an entire new generation of business cards, which include, but are not limited to: audio business cards; E-electronic business cards; and CD business cards. Some even have photos with talking heads spouting a quick infomercial!

You can choose whatever you like, but, for the sake of a direct mail package or a media kit, it may be wise to include an excellent quality paper card. It will keep your costs down considerably!

Always keep the information simple and to the point. No need to list sixteen different phone numbers on a card, i.e. cellular phone number, car phone number, work number, home number, mother-in-law's number, etc. Believe me, I've seen a lot of business cards over the years. The more numbers on the card, the less impressed I am. It is just information overload. Keep it simple!

Business cards are meant to be effective advertising and marketing tools. No matter how techno-weeny (did I just invent another word?) this world gets, handing out your business card may just still be one of the easiest and quickest ways to increase your business!

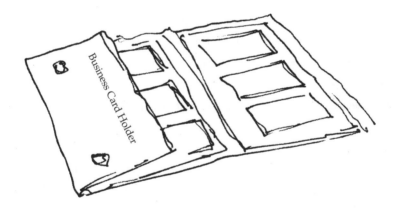

# BROCHURES
## Who could ask for anything more?

Your brochure can speak volumes about you and your Family Life Education programs. As one of your most important marketing tools, it deserves the time to be well designed and well written.

The traditional, folded format provides you with six, perfectly-sized, individual units of space to allow you to organize and present your information in a clear, structured, yet flowing manner. Because of this, a brochure can hold more details and more information than a flier can. There should be no seconding-guessing as to what you are offering.

Brochures are ideal for direct mailings, but don't limit yourself there! Display them in appropriate public places, such as dentists' or doctors' offices, schools, daycare centers, even your place of worship - always be sure to have permission first.

Don't run the risk of your brochures being carelessly scattered around, or falling unnoticed to the floor, or worse still, ending up in the waste basket. Invest in several inexpensive, acrylic brochure holders. This way, your brochures are neatly displayed. Like vending machines, these brochure holders must be checked and refilled periodically.

> To be a successful Family Life Educator, you have to increase your *visibility* and *marketability* in the community.

There are several formats for writing a brochure, each one differing slightly from the other. Experiment. Let a good eye, logical sequence, and a good dose of common-sense be your guide. It may take a few trial runs, but you'll get the hang of it soon enough.

Keep in mind that your brochure is not written in stone. I can assure you that until you create "the right" brochure for *your* target audience, you will be updating and revising it a few times. Don't print them up by the thousands yet. You may end up with expensive scrap paper!

*Much like people -- brochures are always "in process."*

Over the years, I have had the opportunity to see thousands of different brochures. A few stand out in my mind, while others were tossed away. Why? Three basic reasons:

1. The message was not clear, nor well-thought out.
2. Writing style and language weren't conducive to making that necessary connection to the targeted audience.
3. Benefits and features were not mentioned.

Remember that you want to create an impression. You want to have a professional image - your brochure is one of your most effective marketing tools; it identifies you and your programs.

*(Lesson: What does your brochure say about you?)*

# FLIERS

With minimal cost, these *one-page wonders* can attract a lot of attention to your Family Life Education programs. With the use of computer software, clip art and your own imagination, you can put together an effective marketing and advertising tool.

## Headlines

These should be *attention grabbers* - something that the targeted audience can immediately associate with. Headlines in the form of a question work well.

## Text

Clear, concise, understandable language. Make your point- don't overload information.

## Fonts

There is no need to use your computer's entire selection of fonts! This makes text difficult to read (not a good thing to happen!)

## Graphics

An appropriately-sized, subject-related, and eye catching graphic is most appreciated. This helps drive the point home.

## Paper Color

Stay away from colors that are too dark and make your flier hard to read. Bright orange, yellow, lavender, or lime green seem to work well. Experiment with neon colors - see how they look.

## Mini–fliers

I have found mini-fliers to be effective, and cost efficient marketing alternatives, especially when strategically placed in physicians' or dentists' offices, where space is a a premium.

Take a regular 8.5 x 11 inch sheet of paper and copy your reduced text four times on that page.

*(Lesson: Always aim for professionalism--an absolute must on your way to success!)*

# WORD-OF-MOUTH

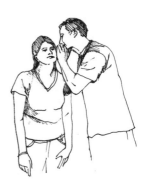

*"Faster than a speeding bullet. More powerful than a locomotive. Able to leap tall buildings in a single bound."*

No, not Superman, but word-of-mouth. Whether in the business community or a circle of friends, nothing spreads faster.

## PRO
Keep your clientele satisfied and they will tell two friends, and so on, and so on. Even though this may be a helpful and inexpensive marketing tool, it is best not to totally rely on it. Choose other back-up methods.

## CON
The down side of this marketing tool is dissatisfaction. In other words, if they are not happy, the news or gossip will spread even faster!

# COLD CALLS

***Brrrrrrrrr!*** If you feel a sudden chill coming over you when thinking of making cold calls - just remember that it is yet another way of reaching your target audience without over extending your budget.

The best way to proceed is to have a script in front of you. It will enable you to stay focused. After the initial pleasantries and information-giving, ask if you can send them a brochure for your upcoming Family Life Education workshop. Start collecting names and addresses. These will be the beginnings of a database.

Expect rejection; it is all part of telemarketing! Be sure to avoid calling anyone around lunch or supper time.

*(Lesson: Like everything else,*
*it gets better with practice!*

How to be a Successful Family Life Educator

# JUST THE FAX, MA'AM

Your Family Life Education program flier may be strategically faxed to your target audience. Faxing is a quick and inexpensive marketing tool. When creating a database list, make sure it is in line with your specific program.

Realistically, your flier may:

- Be directed to the Director's Office
- Be posted on a bulletin board
- Be circulated
- Be taken home by an employee
- Be filed for future reference
- Be put in the trash

You can assure yourself that for a very reasonable cost, you have held the attention of at least one pair of eyes.

When designing your flier, keep in mind that faxes are in black and white. Think about an eye-catching graphic, an interesting bold font, or an appropriate border design along the edge.

Make sure your name and telephone number are clearly visible and on separate lines of text.

# PROMOTIONAL ITEMS

Another way to market yourself and your Family Life Education program is to invest in small, fairly inexpensive promotional items, and distribute them appropriately.

There is no need to dish out thousands of dollars. Some items, such as pens, highlighters, fridge magnets or small adhesive notepads, may all be purchased for under one dollar.

As your budget grows, so can your line of promotional inventory. Mugs (especially traveling-type ones) are always popular. T-shirts are yet another "hot" item.

With a little time, imagination and some computer know-how, you can design and produce your own T-shirts for as little as five dollars each. **Not bad for a personal, walking billboard!**

# NEWSPAPER ADVERTISING

## DISPLAY ADS
There are two types of ads you can buy. The first is often referred to as a Block, Display, or Retail ad. This is the most expensive. You purchase space. Space is measured by the column. Column size is slowly being standardized in the newspaper business.

Width of the ad is determined by the number of columns *across* the page you want. Length is usually in proportion to your ad; and sometimes depends on available space. Keep in mind that Block ads are very often purchased in advance. Sales people like to have you sign a contract, offering you a better deal on rates. As for your preferred spot in the newspaper, well, don't count on this -- it is often what's available, and for the most part, long-standing, large-space-purchasing clients usually get first pick.

Also, prices vary. For instance, a 1/8TH of a page ad in *The New York Times* may be equivalent to the down payment on a home, whereas your local, hometown weekly newspaper may charge you a paycheck for the same size ad.

## CLASSIFIEDS ADS
As the name implies, these ads are for the classified section of a newspaper. Columns are much smaller, and ad space is

bought by number of lines or number of words. Believe me, newspapers have it down to a science -- they can almost tell you how much each word will enhance their profitability!

Classified ads are smaller, but so is the price. The disadvantage is that they are not as "visible" as the larger, display ads (says the salesperson selling advertising space). The choice is ultimately yours. With a little imagination, you can still create a nice ad with the space you buy in the classified section.

**NEWSPAPER ADS:** The Pros and The Cons
First, the good news. Local newspapers usually have a decent circulation. You would naturally assume the more copies "out there," the higher the chances of your ad getting noticed. Now, for the bad news. Your ad is rarely noticed the first few times, which translates into lots of paychecks. You want people to not only notice your ad, but moreover, **respond** to it!

To add insult to injury - the very next day, the same newspaper that has your ad printed (yes, the invested paycheck!) may be used to wrap fish. ***Think about it!***

**AMAZING BUT TRUE!**
On a personal note, I spent many paychecks on newspaper advertising. For months, I tried different sized ads, different fonts, borders, you name it! Yet, I wasn't getting nearly the response I wanted. My advertising budget was depleted. I was devastated. What was I going to do now?

I decided to change my marketing strategy. Remember how I mentioned flexibility and determination? Well, these two qualities kicked in. I suddenly discovered that I could be creative. (Yeah, me.) So, here's what I did. I created a flier, similar to the ad in the newspaper. I scrounged through my desk for paper. The pickings were slim. I had exactly 19 sheets of blue paper, and 16 sheets of yellow paper. Not having much paper, I decided to reduce the size of the flier and place four to a page; hence, the invention of my mini-flier.

I ever so carefully folded the pages in quarters and proceeded to cut them with my late mother's Singer scissors - you know the good ones that are only for cutting fabric?? Well, she was probably rolling in her grave at that point, but I was between a rock and a hard place. Somehow, I knew she would understand.

I gathered up courage, my car keys, and my 140 colorful mini-fliers, and proceeded to distribute them near the check-out counter at convenience and drug stores, and at customer-service desks of grocery stores. Well surprise, surprise. Within 2 weeks, I had **more response** to my mini-fliers than I had with months of big buck display ads in newspapers!!

# INFOMERCIALS

*RADIO and TELEVISION. Are they for you?* You never know until you try. No doubt these are costly advertising strategies, but on the other hand, radio and television are excellent tools. The 30-second spot, enough time for a good infomercial, can help you reach your targeted audience very effectively.

## ABOUT CPM (cost per thousand)

As with newspapers, both radio and tv salespeople will try and push contracts. Keep in mind that their approach is friendly, but very assertive (borderline aggressive??). These fast-talking folks will give you a lot of information - all at once. For instance, they will inform you that newspapers have a *circulation* count, whereas radio has a *listening audience*. And, television will have a *viewing audience*. The salesperson will discuss price -- which will make your jaw drop -- but quickly break price down into CPM (cost per thousand) - then further break it down into cost per person. In effect, they will try to convince you that you can reach your target audience very affordably.

*(Lesson: Negotiate. Negotiate. Negotiate.)*

Don't jump at the first offer. Remember to do *your* homework! Ask questions and get quotes from a few different stations. You might want to ask questions about their

64                       How to be a Successful Family Life Educator

targeted audience and about a match with your own targeted audience. Different people listen at different times and they can suggest time slots. Always keep in mind that you are not purchasing "air time" but audiences. Believe me, they have studied their demographics all right!

## RADIO PERSONALITIES
Family Life Education programs can effectively be advertised on the radio, especially with the help of a radio "personality." Depending on the radio station, the cost may not be more, and you would most definitely benefit from their popularity and perceived credibility.

## THE FREEBIES
### Check your local Chamber of Commerce!
This little tid-bit of information may come in handy, especially since you might consider targeting your audience in an infomercial. Speak to a membership person at your local Chamber of Commerce, and see what is included in a membership package. The last one I looked into **included** several infomercials with popular, local radio stations and a couple of spots on the local cable tv advertising station!

If you had to go out and pay for all of this free broadcast advertising, the cost would come out to more than the membership fee alone. ***This may be an offer you can't refuse.***

# PUBLIC RELATIONS

Ever wonder why some people, organizations or companies always seem to be in the news? Do you really think it just happens by magic? I don't think so. Advertising experts make their living by keeping people in the news, in the forefront, in the public eye.

As a Family Life Educator, you have to be your own advocate. So, start tooting your own horn! Seize every opportunity you can to educate the public, and also let them know how good you really are! (I know, I know ... this is not something that comes easily).

When you are able to do something good for the community, like offering to speak at a community gathering or event, or doing a mini seminar -- write a **press release** about it and tie it to Family Life Education. Make your name, as well as your workshops noteworthy.

Public relations is considered to be:

- the **least expensive** form of advertising
- the **most productive** form of advertising

You can't do better than this 2 for 1 special, can you?

As I did, you might also want to consider establishing and developing a positive relationship with a local newspaper editor. You want your name to be one they remember - and believe me, they will.

One day, I gathered up my courage and decided to make a telephone call to a local newspaper editor. Obviously impressed by what I had to say, she asked me to drop by her office later that week. I gladly agreed, but suddenly, my legs felt so weak I didn't think they could hold me up.

I spent days preparing for this interview. I was ready. I felt great! I was excited, passionate and comfortable talking about Family Life Education and the important role of prevention. I walked into the editor's office and spoke with her as if she was an old friend.

That one, brave, telephone call led to a 1/2-page feature article on Family Life Education, me and the workshops I was offering at the time. The article even included my photo, which was taken by a newspaper staff photographer.

I just want to let you know that people in the Media have the power to help you boost your career; after all, don't you want to be successful as a Family Life Educator?

# THE PRESS RELEASE

Be it newspaper, radio or television, editors working in the Media are under constant pressure to meet deadlines. For these special breed of people, time is of the essence. There is a lot of competition and little time for media staff to read your press release in great detail. Information has to be presented clearly and succinctly; there is no time for second-guessing what you are trying to say.

## TIPS ON WRITING A PRESS RELEASE

- Use white, letterhead stationery.
- Stick to one page in length.
- Type, never handwrite.
- Use double-spacing.
- Leave wide margins.
- Write clearly and concisely.
- Clearly identify contact person's name, telephone and fax number.
- Have a title that grabs attention and makes the reader want to keep reading.
- Three paragraphs should be sufficient: a beginning, middle and end.
- Pique interest in first paragraph.
- Be sure to cover the basic journalism elements: Who? What? When? Where? Why? How?
- Include a relevant quote.
- Provide direct and specific information (don't embellish).
- Unless targeting a specific academic or professional journal, use vocabulary that's free of psycho-jargon.
- Check grammar and spelling for errors.

# MEDIA KITS
## Tired of waiting to get noticed?

Put together a media kit (sometimes known as a press kit) and see what happens! It is an ideal way to introduce yourself to the media. It is an extremely powerful marketing tool that can play an important role in creating and boosting your professional image. After all, you **DO** want the community to know about you and what you can offer them, right?

### WHAT EXACTLY IS IT?

A media kit is a well-put-together packet that contains information on you, the Family Life Educator, and your programs. If your media kit is found to be newsworthy, the possibilities are astounding. Getting noticed by the media is a wonderful way for you to educate the community about Family Life Education **and** get some (free) publicity!

A basic media kit should include the following:
- A cover letter (sometimes called an outreach letter)
- A copy of your press release
- Your brochure
- Your business card

You may want to add these:

   -A short biography

   -A photo (preferably black and white, and professionally taken)

   -A schedule of upcoming workshops

   -A topic or question sheet (this is a way of creating and steering a conversation that may occur at a later date)

   -Reprints of newspaper or magazine articles about you (if available)

## HOW DO YOU PUT ONE TOGETHER?

The answer is - very carefully, with painstaking attention to detail. You want to project a professional image; therefore, you must not skimp on the quality of paper you will be using for your business cards or brochures. I can not stress this point enough - now is not the time to starting counting pennies - buy high quality stationery. Try color-coordinating folders with stationery, but be tasteful about it. You want to attract attention, but not negative attention.

## WHY THE BIG FUSS?

Because you are investing in yourself! Media kits are investments in yourself - each one that you send has a wealth of potential. Professional image is key - and sometimes that costs, but when sending out this kind of information, appearing cheap or sloppy is definitely not an option. Do it right, or don't bother doing it at all!

## WHO DO YOU SEND IT TO?

Media Kits may either be sent or hand-delivered (if possible) to strategic people in the media, such as editors who deal with family-related, work-family or personal development stories or features (not the sports editor!) They can be sent to newspapers, radio stations and television stations. Find out the name of the editor that you are targeting: otherwise, this packet can just be left sitting on someone's desk.

## CHECK IT OVER

Take the extra time to ensure that all material included in your media kits is checked and re-checked for errors in grammar and spelling. Also make every possible effort to make sure they land in the right hands. I prefer to hand deliver my media kits. Even if the editor does not have time to talk with you right away, chances are you will be remembered.

# WORKING WITH THE MEDIA
## Did your media kit get their attention? Great!

One way of staying "visible" in the community, is making an attempt to work hand-in-hand with the media, such as journalists, editors, and radio or television personalities.

Many of my colleagues prefer to keep a low profile, shying away from the media. *However*, how are you to "sell your qualifications" as a Family Life Educator if you don't make an effort to get in the spotlight every once in a while! Yes, it takes courage. Promoting yourself does take determination, competence, perseverance and a lot of *chutzpah!*

Since these media people have little or no time to waste, I strongly suggest that when you deal with these folks - *BE PREPARED*. Know your stuff inside out! Their time is limited, and as a result, their patience, frustration and tolerance levels can sometimes be low. Slightly task-oriented, you say?

Make an effort to see beyond the rushed, hardline media person. They are people too -- complete with families, big hearts and a lot of connections in the business.

*(Lesson: Stop hiding! Go out there and get noticed!)*

*No one can make you*
*feel inferior*
*without your consent.*

*Eleanor Roosevelt*

# "LIGHTS ... CAMERA ... ACTION!
## Welcome to the wonderful world of the media ...

Papers rustling, support staff bustling, journalists, editors, news people hustling ... all for that good feature story to fill a time slot. It's about ratings, numbers, informing and pleasing the public.

It is a never-ending story of constantly having to produce and to meet deadlines. One interview is barely finished, but minds are racing ahead, planning the next two interviews that have to be done by the end of the day.

The media's tried-and-true areas of self-improvement, interpersonal relationships and family-related issues are always being focused on. These are considered to be the Big Three in some media circles. Just think of some of the latest tv talk shows. The content is familiar, but the media, like Family Life Educators, have to be creative when covering those topics. It's the much talked about "angle" or perspective. Sound familiar?

If your media kit is noticed, you may get more attention than you're looking for. Goodness knows, I've certainly had my share. Whether it's the press, radio or television, the experience can best be described as having two opposing feelings happening at the same time. On the one hand, it's exciting, energizing, exhilarating! On the other hand, it is anxiety-provoking and terrifying.

## TELEVISION

This is big-time, baby. Not much room for the faint of heart, nor weak in the knees. Being able to think on your feet is a definite asset. Take my word on this one. I have been interviewed on several occasions, but my very first interview was one that I shall never forget.

I was so intrigued by everything! The doting staff, the celebrity host, the make-up room, the cameras with their blinking red lights, the at-home looking "stage" that stood alone in a very large, otherwise barren room, the extra bright lights and the never-ending flow of questions I was obliged to answer.

For the most part, television shows are taped in advance; however, this particular local talk-show host, preferred to do his interviews live. Furthermore (and unbeknown to me), he had a flair for asking the most irrelevant questions. (Do you see where this is going?)

Yes, like all the hundred of guests before me, he also threw me a curve ball -- asking something about the legislative procedure involved in getting a certain bill put into effect. Although I knew about the bill he was referring to, I most certainly did not have the details on the government procedures he wanted to know about. Nor did it really matter; he was way off topic here, and he knew it. But, I was the one who was stumped. To make matters worse -- I was on *live* television.

Well, it was only a matter of five seconds or so before I responded, but, at that very moment, it seemed like a veritable eternity. I can truly say this was one of the most terrifying moments of my life.

To make matters even worse, he repeated his question. He looked at me for an answer. My face wore a pensive expression (sure, it was pensive - I was wracking my brain for an answer. Also, I was plea-bargaining with God!)

Then, it hit me. I played him at his own game. I looked directly at him and said that these details were of trivial importance, and that the real issue was the needs of families. I continued to say that we had to focus on "the why" of that law, not "the how" - then I offered my brightest smile. Yes, folks, I turned the tables on him.

*(Lesson: Know your stuff! Be prepared for the unexpected!)*

Even though your stomach may be in knots, try and appear relaxed, and don't forget to smile  - after all, you do want to look approachable. (I know it's difficult when the foremost thing on your mind is that it may go blank from stage fright.)

On a lighter note, let the make-up artists work their magic. Believe me, you may even want to take one home with you. They are experts at making the dark circles under your eyes disappear.

As far as clothing is concerned, go for the professional look. However, it is best to avoid wearing black - the on-camera look is very severe. Also, stay away from clothes that are uncomfortable and that limit your ability to move. Believe me, at some point you'll want to shift your weight around in your chair, and you can't be tugging at your clothes or fidgeting. Whatever you do, don't wear wool suits, or heavy sweaters. You will regret doing so. The "stage" has very powerful lights, and room temperatures can soar to over 100 degrees. You way also want to be aware of strategically placed and highly-sensitive microphones. Try not to wear heavy metal bracelets or clinking bangles - the sound will be picked up quickly and might detract from the interview. As for reminder notes, keep them to one or two index cards that could be discretely used.

How do I know all this? For my second television interview, I wore a fitted, black, wool dress with long sleeves and a high-neck collar. I was extremely warm and very uncomfortable. Sweat was running down my back. Although my jewelry was tasteful for the outfit, the heavy gold bracelet "clanked" every time I put my hand back down on the desk after gesturing. Also, because I was still slightly nervous, I kept relying on my notes. Luckily, this was not too noticeable; I quickly figured out the rhythm of the camera shots, and when it was focusing on the interviewer I sneaked a peek at my notes.

*Experience is not what
happens to a man.
It is what a man does
with what happens to him.*

**Aldous Huxley**

# THE SPOTLIGHT IS ON YOU ...
## TAKE FULL ADVANTAGE
## OF THIS OPPORTUNITY TO
## EDUCATE THE COMMUNITY

### RADIO INTERVIEWS

These are a piece of cake compared to the television interviews! Since you will be heard and not seen, your voice is one of your most important and effective tools. From my experience, many of the personalities are a little easier to work with, perhaps because the entire scenario and entourage is less formal in nature than television.

Informal or not, you *still* have to project professionalism. You *still* have to know your stuff inside out. As with television, be prepared for the unexpected, as you never know what tricks lie up the interviewer's sleeve.

Remember the topic or question sheet that I previously mentioned  in the section on Media Kits? This is where it comes into play. I have found that by using this prepared sheet, you stand a good chance of creating and steering a conversation where you want it to go. Make 2 copies - one for yourself and one for the radio personality. It clearly out-lines the limits and boundaries you wish to abide by during the interview. The interviewer will catch on quickly enough.

Be sure to pause briefly after a question is asked of you. It has to sound like you are thinking about the question and giving appropriate thought to your answer. Be certain that you don't interrupt the interviewer. This sounds horrible on-air! Both voices are heard, but sometimes cannot be distinguished one from the other, and confusion sets in.

You are free to bring a few notes, but you don't want to sound like you are reading a script either. Also, keep in mind that the microphones are extremely sensitive and that every rustling sound will be heard. After a couple of interviews, you will be a pro.

After trying out some of these marketing strategies, you will quickly discover what works best for you, as you promote Family Life Education. Be warned! You may get a sudden influx of calls as a result of either a newspaper, radio or television interview.

*"On-air in five, four, three, two, one!"*

How to be a Successful Family Life Educator

Part Three

# EDUCATING THE COMMUNITY

There are several ways to educate the community about Family Life Education and the programs you and your agency have to offer. It is important to realize that some of the most effective methods involve actually getting out there and taking an active role in the process.

*Are you ready? Good. Then, let's get started!*
*I'll talk you through each step of the way.*

# PUBLIC SPEAKING ENGAGEMENTS
## --You're The Expert

Are you a:
- Member of a community-based club?
- Board Member of a community or non-profit organization?
- Member of the sisterhood in your local place of worship?
- Volunteer at the Ladies Auxiliary of the local hospital?
- Member of the P.T.A.?

This is an excellent way to educate the community! As a Family Life Educator, you are most definitely knowledgeable about families. And, just about everybody has a family, so you're in luck! As the expert in your field, you may be called upon, or better still, *OFFER* to do a public speaking engagement in the community.

Specific family-related areas that require either problem-solving or coping skills may in fact be of interest to many members of the community. They may appreciate knowing there is help out there that is non-threatening, supportive, and *p-r-e-v-e-n-t-i-v-e* in nature. They also may be thankful that they don't have to wait to be in a crisis situation in order for them to address or resolve pressing issues.

Your goals are to educate and promote. As an expert in your field, you are creating an impression. Let your passion and enthusiasm shine through. Professionalism is at the forefront. Keep in mind that for the most part, you will be speaking to individuals who are active in the community. These people network with other individuals in and around the community.

Here is a guideline with important key points to keep in mind when speaking:

### About Family Life Education
- Have a smooth, short, comfortable working definition prepared when speaking about Family Life Education.
- Give an overview of the wide-range of ages, stages, topic areas and content covered.
- If you are certified by either the National Council on Family Relations or Family Service Canada, be sure to mention the stringent criteria that these organizations require in order to certify a person. You may want to distribute some of the NCFR brochures on "Hiring?" which explains Family Life Education and certification to employers.

### About Prevention and the Important Role It Plays
- How life's stressors can take their toll on an individual over time.
- How individuals cope better when life's issues are addressed in a timely and effective manner.
- Mention the medical model and the tendency to wait until a crisis happens.
- How there are fewer visits to Doctors' offices and Emergency Rooms when people consider changing to a more prevention-oriented mindset.

- The correlation between a decrease in percentage of non-urgent cases, and a resulting decrease in waiting room time.
- The bottom line, millions of healthcare tax dollars saved when both Americans and Canadians change to a healthier, preventive-oriented lifestyle.
- In conclusion, it may in fact prove to be more cost-efficient and cost-effective for government and businesses to hire Family Life Educators to assist individuals with basic interpersonal, communication and coping skills.

## Professionalism

- Have a good supply of your business cards and brochures.
- Be prepared to answer questions both during and after your speech, as people will most likely approach you.
- Project a professional image (dress and act appropriately).

## Attitude and Body Language

- Be respectful.
- Keep a positive attitude at all times.
- Use body language that says "confidence."
- Last, but not least, **keep breathing!**

If you would like to build your confidence as a public speaker, I strongly suggest that you contact ToastMasters International. They are world-renown for their training programs.

Whether your topic is "Engaging Cooperation In Children" or "The Pros and Cons of Retirement," you must be relaxed and enthusiastic about your program.

When it comes to promoting the field of Family Life Education, and your programs, your own personality and effective communication style are your most important keys to **successful marketing**!

# NETWORKING: SCHMOOZE OR LOSE
## Are you, your agency or organization a member of the local Chamber of Commerce?

If so, make an effort to attend one of their regularly sched-uled "Business After Hours" networking events. You may even ask permission to attend. For the most part, the membership person will be very obliging and will most probably invite you to participate (as long as you say that you are considering becoming a member, and just want to get an idea of what these get-togethers are like).

These evenings are specifically designed for business members in the community. In an informal, more relaxed, social-type setting, they provide business members the opportunity to:

- Learn about other businesses in the community.
- Meet new people.
- Make important contacts.
- Exchange information.
- Strengthen the business community at large.

### KEEPING TRACK OF WHO's WHO
Smile and do a business card exchange. Invest in a business cardholder. You will be amazed at the number of cards you will soon collect.

How to be a Successful Family Life Educator

A handy little trick that I use is to write comments on the back of each card I receive. This not only helps in remembering who is who, but also serves to trigger key points that you can use later. For example: "Man in brown suit. Staff Development Officer. Send info on Stress Management."

## STAYING FOCUSED

Remember, you are on a "mission" with very specific goals in mind. Your duties are to:

- Make a positive impression.
- Gather information from more than one person.
- Disseminate information on Family Life.
  Education and its programs.
- Make contacts.

## ATTITUDE AND PROFESSIONALISM

Project a professional image. Dress for success and act appropriately. Just walk into the room with a positive and friendly attitude and mingle! Stay away from the hors d'oeuvres and alcoholic refreshments. For the next hour or so, your mouth will be reserved for talking - you need to be alert and not have spinach on your teeth.

Take full advantage of this networking event. It's your perfect opportunity to get to know more about the various businesses in your community. Speak with other guests and ask appropriate questions. Do a quick little survey. For instance, ask about the size of the company, its location, and how long they've been in business. Then, move on to more specific questions concerning staff.

Always keep in mind that answers may differ and opinions may vary, depending on who is talking; support staff or management. Some people have an easier time talking than others. From my experience, open-ended questions are best. As you may agree, there are people who love to talk, especially about themselves!

## SUPPORT STAFF

If you are speaking with support staff, ask questions like these:

- What exactly they do in the company?
- Do most employees fall into a certain age category?
- In their opinion, what are the top three family-related issues that co-workers seem to be having a problem with recently? Is it parenting issues, dealing with aging parents, finances, interpersonal relationships, stress, or some other issue?
- A gem of a question is asking the person to describe the relationship between employees and management. The answer to this question will equip you with much insight about the inside of the company and how it operates.
- An excellent question is finding out who has the power inside the company - the real power. The answer may surprise you!

## MANAGEMENT

On the other hand, if you happen to be speaking with management, you will most probably get an entirely different perspective. Ask them to describe these:

- The "employee-management relationship".
- Their management style.
- The major employee-related concerns. Is it substance abuse? Family-Work balance related issues? An increase in absenteeism?

Perhaps mention that you recently read an interesting article in 'us.chamber.com' (which is the U.S. Chamber of Commerce's monthly publication). This publication features articles on business, growth and image. Let's just say that image is very important - companies want to be perceived as the good guys. As a result, there is an increasing trend in companies tuning in to the trend of helping employees - sometimes in areas like better balancing the demands of work and family. (Enough said.)

## THE WRAP UP

Then, move on to some final questions. Inquire if their company has a newsletter, and if so, how often it is published. Ask if they have ever considered offering workshops, brown-bag lunch seminars, or other on-site training. Ask if they would be interested in receiving an information package on the various programs you offer.

The answers to these questions will help you discern which companies to target for your Family Life Programs.

*(Lesson: Work it Baby, work it!)*

# THE BUSINESS COMMUNITY
## .. You're Playing with the Big Boys, Now!

*All right. You've decided that Company XYZ is included in your list of companies to target. Now what happens?*

## THE FOLLOW-UP

That's simple enough. If you met one of the company managers as a result of a speaking engagement or a Chamber of Commerce event, be sure to quickly follow through with an "It was nice meeting you note." Include some brochures on the Family Life Education program(s) you offer. Give them about a week; then follow up with a telephone call and schedule a meeting.

## PLAYING HARDBALL

When you do meet, I suggest you be prepared! You have your foot in the door; now you have to negotiate with company executives. Definitely not a walk in the park. This is tougher. You had better know your stuff and have several years' experience under your belt. Equip yourself with a soft sell. Companies will want to "talk turkey." They will want to know specific information:

1) What can you do for them?
2) How do you plan on doing it?
3) Why should they hire you?
4) What's it going to cost them?

## ON WITH THE SHOW

Keep in mind that they are now sitting behind their desk, and they are in a position to ask *you* the questions. This can be intimidating unless you have some prepared answers. Here is your chance to educate the business community on how Family Life Education programs can help.

## APPEALING TO THEIR SOFT SIDE

Companies hire employees. These employees are individuals and usually have families. There are often family-related issues to be addressed and worked out. Sometimes, there are difficult family decisions or issues to be addressed that weigh heavily on an employee's shoulders. Often employees require education, or coping skills. The reality is that sometimes these issues affect the employees' work performance -- sometimes, we all need a helping hand -- after all, don't we all have families? The very goals of Family Life Education and its programs are preventive in nature, and that is a plus in itself. The quote "An ounce of prevention is worth a pound of cure" might be appropriate to use now. Stress how the employee will have the opportunity to help him/herself in the workshop or program that you would like to offer.

## CUT TO THE CHASE

Try this approach of explaining it in terms of an equation. Family-Work issues are a big concern for companies. Why? Simply because they often affect an employee's work performance in terms of productivity and/or absenteeism. Employees who feel they have more of a sense of control over their lives are better workers. Better workers produce better results. Better results mean increased efficiency and effectiveness, which translates into more profits. More profits make everyone happy. All people love to hear about the features and benefits. It's a selling job, no doubt, but it may not be as difficult as you think.

In the past decade, several articles have been written in *The Wall Street Journal* and *Business Week* about family needs in the workforce. They claim that most managers are aware of and sensitive to the fact that the workforce is changing to include millions of single moms and single dads. As a result, these managers are realizing that programs that respond to family needs and the work-family balancing act are no longer considered a luxury, but a fact of life in competitive companies. They believe that family-friendly companies will target, attract and keep the best workers.

## THE WRAP-UP

So, in effect, the Family Life Education programs you are offering are invaluable to the company. It's a win-win situation. Quickly follow-up by asking when they would like to schedule the first series of workshops, and offer them a choice of specific dates.

*(Lesson: Think BIG. You won't realize your potential until you do.)*

# TRY YOUR HAND AT WRITING

Contributing to your local newspaper is another way of reaching, educating and sharing with your community. The benefit for you is that your name and/or organization will appear in subscribers' homes, and the wonderful part about that is you don't even have to pay to get it there! But always remember that your primary goal is to connect with the community.

You might want to consider one of the following:

## LETTER TO THE EDITOR
By taking the time and initiative to respond to a recent news article, be it a feature article or an item from the lifestyle section, on children or even some pending legislation, you have the perfect opportunity not only to express your learned opinion, but also to tie in your area of expertise. Use clear and concise language, and you might want to provide some easy-to-understand statistics for the sake of comparison. Don't forget to make your conclusion as thought-provoking as possible - you want your readers to think.

## CHILD OR FAMILY RELATED  FEATURE ARTICLE
What's your area of expertise?  Parenting?  Young Children?  Adolescents? Mid-Life Crisis?
The Fabulous Fifty crowd?  The Sexy Seniors?

Newspapers are always looking for fresh approaches and different angles to keep their readers' interest. You might want to consider writing a feature story from a different perspective. Provide some quotes and some statistics; then if possible, link it to some recent event in the community.

The readers must feel that you are approachable. And you want to be. Perhaps you can conclude your story by inviting them to attend one of your programs. This gives the readers the opportunity to get to know you via your story. If they like what they read, chances are you will most probably see them at your workshop.

## OFFER TO WRITE A COLUMN

I'm not kidding; you could do it! Here's another great way of not only educating the community, but also getting them involved. People love to write to the experts - it's their way of getting help for free. Seriously, it's a wonderful way to connect. Who better to answer questions on communication and interpersonal skills than you, the Family Life Educator. And who knows? You may even be picked up by other newspapers and have a syndicated column like Dear Abby

Remember what I said about thinking out-of-the-box? It's a simple recipe: 1/3 imagination, 1/3 creativity, 1/3 believing in yourself! The last ingredient is one of the most important ones in being a *successful* Family Life Educator.

# YOUR TARGET AUDIENCE:
## ...HOW TO KEEP 'EM!

*What's the best way to find something out?  Ask. Just Ask*!
Whether it's taking surveys at the beginning or at a
mid-way point of an eight-week program, or doing evaluations
at the end - the data you compile will be priceless.  After all,
you are aiming at increasing your effectiveness.

As an incentive to completing evaluations, you may even
consider rewarding participants' efforts with an appropriate
token of appreciation, such as a discount coupon, which can
be applied towards any of your upcoming workshops! (We
do live in a consumer society where people believe they
should be rewarded for purchases.)

Yes, it's back to number crunching! This is not only an
excellent method of tracking your progress, but also finding
out more about what participants want and need. Take the
time to really get to know your target audience. Be sure to
**carefully consider** their suggestions for improvement, and
**act upon them**. As a skilled Family Life practitioner, you are
equipped with skills, flexibility and knowledge. Therefore,
fine-tweaking your program to better suit the needs of your
client should not be too difficult.

## Seven Strategies To Success

When it comes to keeping your target audience coming back for more, follow these strategies:

1.  Never take your workshop participants for granted.
2.  Give them more than expected.
3.  Be professional.
4.  Keep up with the latest trends and changes in your topic area.
5.  Keep them happy.
6.  Keep in touch afterwards
7.  Offer discount coupons that can be applied towards your next workshop!

Your goal is more than just getting your name out there. It's about satisfying your audience before, during and after your program. In effect, it is the human side of "customer knowledge" that has to be captured, in order for you, the Family Life Educator, to be *successful*.

> *(Lesson: Your evaluations are a good resource tool for improving your program to better suit group participants.)*

# Never Give Any Less
# Than Your Personal Best!

Part Four

# FAMILY LIFE EDUCATORS
# ARE PEOPLE TOO!

Now that you have been equipped with the detailed guidelines of educating the community, working with the media, finding and keeping your target audience, and other marketing and advertising tools and strategies, promoting yourself as a Family Life Educator is no longer shrouded in mystery.

There is still one important area to cover. And that, my fellow Family Life Educators, is YOU. You undoubtedly wear many hats, and change them often during the day. As a Family Life Educator, you have chosen a profession that is still struggling with issues of identity and recognition.

To get ahead in this profession, you must be actively involved in promoting yourself and your programs. These additional tasks may prove to be demanding - and you may find your hat collection  growing! The level of success you achieve may be in direct proportion to the amount of hands-on experience you devote to the various facets of Family Life Education.

In this business of helping others, you can easily forget to help yourself. You too, are an individual, with your own set of needs and issues to be addressed. The next few pages are devoted to you, the Educator, the Person.

Over the past few years, I've had more than my share of "roadblocks," and it took much persistence and determination not to get too sidetracked. Life is short - take the time to laugh at your own quirks and resistance. Therefore, I would like to take this opportunity to provide you with a light-hearted approach to a few key guidelines that may help you overcome some of those same roadblocks on your path to success as a Family Life Educator.

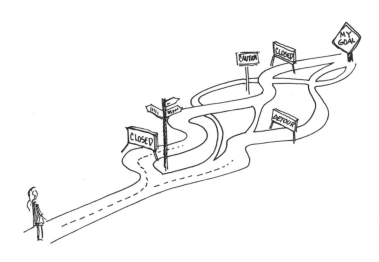

After a while you learn
the subtle difference between
holding a hand and chaining a soul
and you learn that love
doesn't mean leaning
and company doesn't always mean security.
And you begin to learn
that kisses aren't contracts and
presents aren't promises
and you begin to accept
your defeats with your head up
and your eyes ahead
with the grace of a woman
not the grief of a child
and you learn to build all your roads on today
because tomorrow's ground is
too uncertain for plans
and futures have a way of falling down in mid–flight.
After a while you learn
that even sunshine burns
if you get too much
so you plant your own garden
and decorate your own soul instead of waiting
for someone to bring you flowers
And you learn that you really can endure
that you really are strong
that you really do have worth
and you learn
and you learn
with every goodbye you learn.

Author Unknown

# THE IMPORTANCE OF TAKING CARE OF YOUR OWN NEEDS

So, you're a Family Life Educator, huh? You know all about "needs" and that kind of stuff, right? You must have studied this Maslow guy somewhere along the line, and you must really understand his hierarchy on needs. Wow! I'm really impressed.

Hey you! Yeah you, the smart one over there! Are you aware that **your own needs** have to be fulfilled? I'm talking about your personal needs and your emotional needs; are they left to sit quietly on the shelf? Are they pushed into a corner, with a hope and promise to eventually get to fulfilling them? You have great intentions. You are great at helping your clients, **BUT** ... do you have a tendency to let your own stuff go, wishing it would all just magically disappear?

Sometimes, life has a way of taking care of itself - things have a way of working themselves out - and, sometimes not. It is imperative for you to adopt a positive attitude. But, how the heck do you do that? Simple. Recognizing the fact that you have to take care of your own needs. It is only in fulfilling your own personal or emotional needs that you truly find yourself in an even better position to help others. It is only when you can belong, advance, achieve and receive recognition for your efforts, can you feel secure.

Once you feel secure and content, and are not totally focused on having your basic personal and emotional needs met, then you can "allow" that stimulating, energetic flow of creativity to shape you and your work as a Family Life Educator.

*(Lesson: Dare to be creative! Dare to be the best you can be! Why? Because you owe it to yourself, because you deserve it, and you are darn well worth it, baby!)*

## "WHEN YOU ALLOW YOURSELF
## TO THINK OUT-OF-THE-BOX,
## THE POSSIBILITIES ARE LIMITLESS!"

*Rocco Petruolo*

# See Change as an Opportunity for Growth

Psst! Wanna hear a scary word? The one thing that most of us have in common is a dread for **change**. Yes, that dirty little word that you speak about in your workshops, but sometimes, like your clients, you cringe at the very thought of. Many times, your fears get in the way of problem-solving. Without realizing it, you become your own worst enemy. Why? It's actually quite simple: you don't like change. Period.

Change is a normal process and should be regarded as an opportunity for growth. At times, you would rather wallow in your misery than attempt to change the way you react to someone or something. It's the nature of human beings. You tend to keep old habits, rather than develop new ways of coping or dealing with a situation or issue. Even though your old coping strategies are no longer as effective as you would like them to be, you tend to desperately cling to them, rather than try a new or different way of coping. Why? Because these old ways are comforting to you. How are they comforting? Simply, because they are familiar.

You have to take an active role in pushing yourself out of your comfort zone - a place where if you really look, isn't so comfortable anymore. Don't stifle your creativity. When your creativity is decreased, you may find that your level of frustration increases. The good news is, you don't have to do all these changes in one day. Your own self-esteem is not a constant; it has a tendency to fluctuate and much like the ocean, it ebbs and tides.

*(Lesson: Change is different. Change is good; it can lead to a better life. Try it, you may like it!)*

# The Dilemma

"To laugh is to risk appearing a fool.
To weep is to risk appearing sentimental.
To reach out for another is to risk involvement.
To expose feelings is to risk rejection.
To place your dreams before the crowd is to risk ridicule.
To love is to risk not being loved in return.
To go forward in the face of overwhelming odds
is to risk failure.

But risks must be taken because the greatest hazard in life is to risk nothing. The person who risks nothing does nothing, has nothing, is nothing. He may avoid suffering and sorrow, but he cannot learn, feel, change, grow or love.  Only a person who risks is free."

Author Unknown

How to be a Successful Family Life Educator

# STILL AFRAID TO TAKE A RISK?

Do the words *"fight or flight" ring a bell?*
Scared to take a risk?  Okay, I know, I know. You're anxious, and start getting this queasy feeling way down in your guts. You would rather be someplace else ... anyplace else. You just don't want to do it. Ask yourself, what is so terrible about what you have to face? Why are you so scared? What's the worst case scenario?  Will the sky fall in? Will the world come to an end?  *I don't think so!*

You spend way too much valuable time worrying about a fantasized negative outcome. Very rarely are things as bad as you imagine them to be. Go on -  at least take a well-calculated risk at first. Then, with that under your belt, you should have the confidence to attempt another.  As the saying goes, you have nothing to fear but fear itself.

*(Lesson: So be adventurous, take a chance, take a risk. You may be glad you did!)*

# GOALS ARE VISIONS

# THAT WE TURN

# INTO REALITIES.

# GOT GOALS?

Where do you see yourself in two years? Five years? Are you more recognized in the community? Do you have a dynamite program? Have you experienced media attention yet? These may be among your goals as a Family Life Educator.

Regardless of what your goal, plan, or dream is, you have to write it down. Whether it's on your calendar, in your agenda, on your fridge, in a journal or diary, or on a giant poster in your room, remember to always write your ideas down. They can be written in key words, point form, paragraphs, diagrams, flow-charts, organigrams, doodles or stickmen -- just put them down! You will not only remember your ideas, but you will have committed yourself to them by actually having them down on paper.

For example, this very book is the culmination of 84 multi-colored, multi-sized, scribbled Post-it notes; 25 napkins (from fast-food chains); and 14 torn envelopes (from electricity or phone bills). *I kid you not!*

# PLAY AN ACTIVE ROLE

# IN CREATING

# YOUR DESTINY.

# CREATING AN ACTION PLAN

***It's all in the plan!***

You've committed yourself by writing your goals down. But that commitment just doesn't materialize without you being an ACTIVE participant. That's right, you have to make it happen! Always remember that nothing is beyond your reach if you want it badly enough. (By the way, I've kept all the above scraps of paper as a reminder of this book as proof.)

So how do you become an active participant? By getting off your tush! That's right, you heard me. You may be totally exhausted from planning and working on your strategies, plans and dreams. Yes, it's hard work, I know. BUT, honestly, it has to happen somewhere else besides just in your head.

The reality here is that unless you actually DO something concrete about accomplishing your goals, you won't be any closer than you were six months ago. The interesting part is, if you don't, I can assure you that you will still be as tired and frustrated as always. So tell me, what do you have to lose?

You have to plan backward, and work forward. This just means know what you want to achieve, and then work your way toward that goal. From personal experience, I know that this is a more efficient and effective process, since you start out knowing what you want to accomplish from the very beginning. Stay focused.

Any positive action, no matter how small, is still a step in the right direction. You will derive much pleasure from actualizing each step, getting closer to your goal. You will establish a solid foundation on which to build.

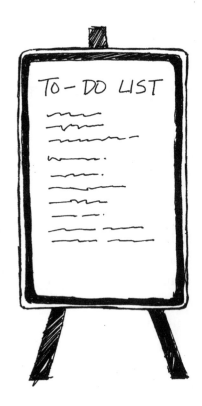

*WHEN FACED WITH A NEW*

*CHALLENGE,*

*DON'T MAKE FEAR*

*THE MAIN EVENT.*

*Rocco Petruolo*

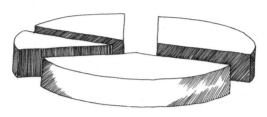

# BREAKING IT DOWN

***Getting unstuck!*** So you have a good idea of what you want to do. But now, you're stuck at some point along the way. When you divide a problem into smaller, manageable parts, you allow yourself to focus on each area separately, without feeling totally overwhelmed and ready to give up.

Once you take a logical and rational look at that problematic area (no matter what it is) and complete what needs to be done, ***then, and only then***, are you ready to continue.

Just remember that you are not alone, and you also have choices. Try going on-line, to the library, or even check the yellow pages for names of people who are experts in a particular field. You will soon realize that people are helpful. All you have to do is ask. People are more than willing to share their knowledge and experience. Once you have what you need, the trick is to keep moving forward - don't waste too much time and energy at the drawing board.

> ***(Lesson: Get some answers, see what works for you, then MOVE ON!)***

# THE POWER OF SELF–TALK

***You can do It!*** Your attitude is vital in creating and developing change. By focusing on altering your old debilitating thoughts and replacing them with newer and healthier ones, you can develop the power to change. For instance, as I mentioned in the section on promoting family life education, never in my wildest dreams did I think I was creative or had imagination. Everyone else seemed to be able to "pull things together" -- and me? Well, I could never do ***THAT!*** (So I thought.) But, the reality was I couldn't because I had convinced myself of such. The problem was, I had not yet learned to ***think out-of-the-box!*** I couldn't see "the big picture".

How often have you heard yourself spout anxious, negative statements, like "I hate this stupid profession! No one even knows what it is!" or "How do I promote something that people don't understand?" or "I can't do this ... I just can't, so why even bother?" So what! Somewhere along the line, like most people I know, you might have a negative experience - I've got news for you, we all have. But, you shouldn't let those negative past experiences stop you.

This is a perfect example of how programmed, negative thought-patterns are our "roadblocks." You sometimes feel doomed before you even begin, thereby actualizing a self-fulfilling prophecy. You have a tendency to give up too easily before you even give yourself a chance to try.

Try some positive "self-talk." It enhances, renews and re-energizes your spirit. You will soon realize that seeing life from a more positive perspective does indeed have its benefits. A weight will be lifted from your shoulders and you will feel alive again. You will suddenly notice that doors and windows of opportunities and accomplishment are open to you. (It is interesting to note that these same doors and windows were actually always around, but you never noticed them before.) Your mind was elsewhere ... busy detouring.

## Certain Things in Life Should Never Be Compromised.

# TIME: A PRECIOUS RESOURCE

*Have ya got some spare time? Yeah, right!* Do you find that there are never enough hours in a day to accomplish what you want? Time is one of the most precious resources we have. Once it is used, it's gone - we cannot get it back. We're all given 24 hours everyday. The choices we make dictate the lives we lead. So choose wisely.

Want to be more in control of your time and; thereby, your life? Try this simple technique for one week. Using a daily planner or a plain sheet of paper, keep track of *every* hour, writing everything down. By the end of the week you will have figured out where your time goes, especially the after-work time.

## AT THE WORKPLACE

Are you like most people, allowing telephone calls, clutter, and unnecessary paperwork to take up your time? Re-organizing your day might save you a couple of hours. Everything in life has a rhythm and generally works in cycles, so find out what time of the day you are most productive (usually mornings) and do the most demanding work or the bulk of your work during that time. Your afternoons will then be freed up to do lighter duties. You will find you will not be as tired when you come home.

## ON THE HOMEFRONT

Sometimes, more time is wasted at home than we would like to think. For the most part, we all have supper to make and laundry to do. Be honest though, now that you have an inventory of your time, did you find that hours were squandered by things like aimlessly surfing the net? (Will your life be at such a loss if you don't keep up with the gossip and trivialities?) Or reading and re-routing e-mail jokes that have already circled the world twice over? Or watching mindless sit-coms or re-runs of re-runs? Or yakking on the phone? Or renting three movies per night?

Each of these activities plays a role in your life (either entertainment, diversion or escape), but you may wish to exercise some restraint. After analyzing my days and how my time was spent, I realized that I wasted about three hours per night just reading e-mail jokes and surfing the net. No one was forcing me to stay on-line for so many hours. I decided to take back control and use my time wisely.

The results were just amazing. In that "saved time" I managed to:

- Design a workshop entitled *How To Be A $uccessful Family Life Educator: Promoting Yourself and Your Programs*, which is approved for 4 Contact Hours by the NCFR.

- Expand that workshop into a book with the same title (Yes folks, the very one you're reading now!)

• Design another workshop entitled ***How To Be a $uccessful Family Life Educator Entrepreneur,*** which is also approved for 6 Contact Hours by the NCFR.

• Create a newsletter entitled: *Flex change* (Family Life Educators Exchange)

• Start my own business, called **FLECT** (Family Life Education, Consultation and Training)

***(Lesson: So, ask yourself this, if you are not in control of your time and your life, then who the heck is?)***

# CELEBRATE EACH SUCCESS

*"Celebrate ....celebrate .... dance to the music!"*
Take time to celebrate and enjoy life! Enjoy your children, for they are your greatest accomplishments.

When it comes to promoting the field of Family Life Education, yourself and your programs, think **SUCCESS**. Keep in mind that you are making a positive and much needed contribution to society.

Celebrate each positive action, each victory, no matter how small or insignificant you may think it is. They will eventually all add up. You may choose to attend a Chamber of Commerce event one week, then contact a media person the following week. You don't have to do it all at once; take one step at a time. Remember that wars are not won all at once, but a battle at a time. Be proud of your profession, of yourself and of the programs you offer.

*(Lesson: Believe in your ability to succeed.)*

# CONCLUSION

We live in a highly complex, always-stressed, and forever-changing society. Families are increasingly diverse in nature, each with its own set of needs and issues to be addressed. Because we are dealing with individuals and families in such a changing world, I truly believe Family Life Education is needed now more than ever before. Our work is definitely cut out for us, as we continue to promote healthy interaction among family members.

Communication, interpersonal relations, coping skills and building self-esteem are all vital ingredients that contribute to the making of strong and healthy families. Without a doubt, strong families (regardless of their composition) are fundamental to a community's well-being.

I wish you all joy, inner peace, health and happiness, as you continue to be a beacon of light in your community.

# Selected Bibliography

Arcus, M.E. (1986). Should family life education be required for high school students? An examination of the issues. *Family Relations*, 35, 347-356.

Arcus, M.E., Schvaneveldt, J.D., & Moss, J.J. (1993). The nature of family life education. In M.E. Arcus, J.D. Schvaneveldt, & J.J. Moss (Eds.), *Handbook of family life education* (Vol. 1, pp. 1-25). Newbury Park, CA: Sage.

Arcus, M.E., & Thomas, J. (1993). The nature and practice of family life eduction. In M.E. Arcus, J.D. Schvaneveldt, & J.J. Moss (Eds.), *Handbook of family life education* (Vol. 2, pp. 1-32). Newbury Park, CA: Sage.

Bangs, D.H., Jr. (1998). *The Marketing Planning Guide* (5th Ed.). Chicago: Upstart Publishing Company.

Blanchard, K. (1999). *The Heart of a Leader*. Tulsa: Honor Books.

Bygrave, W. (Ed.). (1997). *The Portable MBA in Entrepreneurship* (2nd Ed.). New York: John Wiley & Sons.

Canadian Institute for Health Information, *National Health Expenditure Trends, 1975-2000.* Health Expenditures.

Cohen, W.A. & Reddick, M.E. (2000). *Marketing Your Small Business.* Deerfield Beach: Made E-Z Products, Inc.

Daft, Richard L. (1996). *Management* (4th Ed.) Orlando, FL: The Dryden Press.

Darling, C.A. (1987). Family life education. In M.B. Sussman & S.K. Steinmetz (Eds.), *Handbook of Marriage and the Family* (pp. 815-833). New York:Plenum.

Doherty, W.J. (1995). Boundaries between parent and family education and family therapy: The levels of family involvement model. *Family Relations*, 44(4), 353-358.

Dumaine, Brian. "Distilled Wisdom: Buddy Can You Paradigm?" *Fortune*, May 15, 1995, 205-206.

Dumaine, Brian. "Why Great Companies Last," *Fortune*, January 16, 1995, 129.

Fiore, Frank. (2001). *e-Marketing Strategies.* Indianapolis: Que.

Greenbaum, I.L. (1993). *The Handbook for Focus Group Research.* New York: Lexington Books.

Gross, P. (1985). *On family life education: For family life educators* (2nd ed., rev.) Montreal, Quebec, Canada: Concordia University Centre for Human Relations and Community Studies.

Hahn, Fred E. & Mangun, Kenneth G. (1997). *Do-it-Yourself Advertising & Promotion* (2nd Ed.). New York: John Wiley and Sons.

Kennedy, D.S. (2000). *The Ultimate Marketing Plan* (2nd Ed.). Holbrook: Adams Media Corporation.

L'Abate, L . (1983). Prevention as a profession: Toward a new conceptual frame of reference. In D.R. Mace (Ed.), *Prevention in family services: Approaches to family therapy and counseling* (pp. 46-52). Beverly Hills, CA: Sage.

Lasher, W. (1994). *The Perfect Business Plan Made Simple.* New York: Doubleday/Made Simple Book.

Maslow, A.H. (1972). *The Farther Reaches of Human Nature.* New York: Penguin Books.

National Center for Health Statistics. (2001). *National Hospital Ambulatory Medical Care Survey: 1999 Emergency Department Summary.* Hyattsville, MD: Author.

National Center for Health Statistics. (2001). *United States Health,* 2000. Washington, DC: U.S. Department of Health and Human Services, Centers for Disease Control and Prevention.

National Council on Family Relations. (1997a). *Framework for life-span family life education* (Rev. ed.). Minneapolis, MN: Author.

National Council on Family Relations. (January 2000). *Standards and Criteria for the Certified Family Life Educator Program.* Minneapolis, MN:Author.

Otte, M. (1998). *Marketing with Speeches and Seminars.* Seattle, W.A.: Zest Press.

Powell, L.H., & Cassidy, D. (2000). *Family Life Education An Introduction.* Mountain View, CA: Mayfield.

Powell, D.R., Breedlove-Williams, C. (1995). The Evaluation of an Employee Self-Care Program. *Health Values,* 19, 17-22.

Powell, D.R. (1995). Controlling Health Care Costs by Controlling Demand. *Human Resource Professional,* 8, 19-22.

Putman, A.O. (1990). *Marketing Your Services.* New York: John Wiley & Sons.

Schwewe, C.D., & Hiam, A. (1998). *The Portable MBA in Marketing.* (2nd Ed.). New York: John Wiley & Sons.

Shenson, H.L. (1990). *How to Develop and Promote Successful Seminars and Workshops.* New York: John Wiley & Sons.

Statistics Canada. Average payment per medical care service, by category of service. *Catalogue no.* 82F0075XCB.

Tichy, N.M., & Stratford, S. (2001). *Control Your Destiny or Someone Else Will.* New York: Harper Collins.

Wakefield, Ted. No Pain, No Gain. *Canadian Business.* January 1993, 50-54.